Wit & Wisdom for a Friend

Mike Yaconelli

LION
Giftlines

*To my friend, Bill McNabb,
who has spent most of his
life teaching me the meaning
of friendship.*

Introduction

A friend is a rarity, an uncommon, priceless gift. Friendship is talked about as though it were a common occurrence, but true friendships are few and far between.

These thoughts are a celebration of friendship and an attempt to unravel the mystery of a friend. When shared, may they serve to deepen and enrich our own friendships.

Friends do life together.

There is no
recrimination when
a friend makes a
mistake, only
empathy.

Friendship is not
a necessity;
it is a gift.

Whoever is in possession of a true friend sees the exact counterpart of his own soul.

CICERO

We think we know ourselves. We know our idiosyncrasies, our weaknesses, our strengths. We know what makes us tick, what is good and bad about us. We believe that because we have lived with ourselves all our lives we know the person who lives within us. But we don't.

That is why we need friends. They know who we are and are not afraid to introduce us to ourselves.

Friendships are not found; they are made. Thank you for being willing to do the work friendship requires. Thank you for making our friendship.

Flaws are our
lifetime companions –
and so are our
friends.

Friendship is the place where we work out our lives with our words.

Friendship is a single soul dwelling in two bodies.

ARISTOTLE

God chooses our relatives; we choose our friends.

The sweet sincerity of joy and peace, which I draw from this alliance with my brother's soul, is the nut itself whereof all nature and all thought is but the husk and shell. Happy is the house that shelters a friend.

EMERSON

Criticism is welcome
among friends,
because friendship
makes truth palatable.

When friends are
separated by time it
doesn't matter
because when they are
together again they
can start where they
left off.

Friendship is the testing ground for growth.

When two people
are true friends
they can speak to
each other in
silence.

Friends always:

- understand your intentions
- know your weaknesses and flaws… all of them
- celebrate your successes
- weep at your failures

Friends never:

- try to fix you
- use you
- embarrass you... at least not when it really matters
- patronize you
- ask you to lend them money

Friendship is the glue that is made stronger by our differences.

Friends are more than team mates, school mates, work mates, ship mates or church mates. Friends are *soul mates*.

Friendship is risky.
If you are not friends,
there is no risk of
betrayal.

Our souls travelled so unitedly together.

MONTAIGNE

Friends can talk forever, but good friends listen.

The idea of
friendship is worthy,
but genuine
friendship is rare.

Friendship is nothing like you see on television or in movies.

Friendship is complicated but dependable, difficult but worthwhile, demanding but exhilarating, irritating but growth-producing, intrusive but welcome.

In short, friendship is one of life's great gifts.

Friendship is a home for your soul.

Friendship is the marriage of the soul.

VOLTAIRE

The real you – the broken, crooked, irregular you – is safe in the presence of a friend.

Friends do not overlook your lopsidedness; they are attracted by it.

Good friends can fight like cats and dogs, argue politics way into the night, disappoint each other, say things they wish they hadn't said, hurt each other's feelings, and never have trouble forgiving and forgetting.

A Prayer

To my friend God.
Thank you that you
don't just love me; you
like me! I know you
love me; you are
supposed to – you're
God. But like me? You
really are my friend.
Amen.

No one should live
without a friend
and, especially, *die*
without a friend.

Friendships have nothing to do with how much money we have, what kind of position we hold, or our status in the community...

...but not taking a bath can test even the best of friendships.

True friendship is an
identity of souls
rarely to be found in
this world.

GHANDI

The essence of friendship is the courage to be ourselves.

The greatest enemy of friendship is not race, economics, ethnic differences or political disagreement. The greatest enemy is busyness.

Never allow busyness to get in the way of friendship.

People we would like to have as our friends:

- mum
- dad
- sister
- brother
- partner
- God
- a good lawyer
- mother-in-law

People we would rather not have as friends:

- our ex mother-in-law
- the person who sacked us
- the person we sacked
- people who have seen us naked (other than our partners)

A good friend never keeps score.

Friends are rare.
I have a friend who says that his goal in life is to have six friends before he dies so they can be his pall bearers.

At forty years old, he still has two to go.

Friendship is like
dancing the tango.
When you both trip
over each other,
you just tango on.

Friendship insures
you will never
be boring.

Jesus didn't make disciples; he made friends who became his disciples.

Be happy with
those who are
happy,
weep with those
who weep.

FROM THE EPISTLE TO THE
ROMANS

A friend is someone
who knows you well
enough that when
you cancel your plans
they don't ask why.

When men are friends they can cry together. When women are friends they can smoke cigars together. In other words, friendship makes it possible for us to be ourselves *comfortably*.

A friend of mine was with his son in hospital while he was dying. Well-meaning friends came to visit with books, advice, tapes, scripture verses and prayers. He wanted them all to leave.

Then a friend who had lost his own child in a tragic accident came by, slid his chair up next to my friend, held on to his hand and said nothing. My friend never wanted him to leave.

If we live our entire
life with just one good
friend, we will die a
wealthy person.

Your constant love is better than life itself.

FROM PSALM 63

I no doubt deserved
my enemies,
but I don't believe I
deserved my friends.

WALT WHITMAN

Who seeks a friend
without a fault
remains without one.

TURKISH SAYING

As well as loving
your enemies,
treat your friends a
little better.

ED HOWE

May the Lord keep an eye on us while we are separated from each other.

FROM THE BOOK OF GENESIS

Published by
Lion Publishing plc
Sandy Lane West, Oxford, England
ISBN 0 7459 3948 1
First edition 1998
10 9 8 7 6 5 4 3 2 1 0

A catalogue record for this book is available from the British Library

Printed and bound in Singapore

Acknowledgments
Scriptures are quoted from the *Good News Bible* published by The Bible Societies/HarperCollins Publishers Ltd., UK, © American Bible Society, 1966, 1971, 1976, 1992
Jacket picture: *At the Window* by K.H.A. Broge, Christie's Images/Bridgeman Art Library, London